I0814172

To my brother Maurizio, who drew animals even on the pizza boxes
—Serenella

“When a single animal species disappears, we have lost it forever.”
—Félix Rodriguez de la Fuente, naturalist and scientific broadcaster

“There is as much educational benefit to be gained from studying captive dolphins as there would be from studying mankind by observing only prisoners in solitary isolation.”
—Jacques-Yves Cousteau, oceanographer and underwater marine biologist

“It is folly to think that we can destroy one species and ecosystem after another and not affect humanity. When we save species, we're actually saving ourselves.”
—Joel Sartore, *National Geographic* wildlife photographer and conservationist

---

Extinctopedia
This edition published in 2024 by Red Comet Press, LLC, Brooklyn, NY
English Translation © 2024 Red Comet Press
Translated by Margaret Greenan
English language edition graphic direction by Michael Yuen-Killick
The Smithsonian name and logo are registered trademarks of the Smithsonian.

Original title: *Estinctopedia*
First published in Italian by Camelozampa © 2022
Original Italian text © 2022 Serenella Quarello
Illustrations © 2022 Alessio Alcini
Scientific review by Marco Ferrari
Original graphic direction by Elisa Bena

All rights reserved. No part of this book may be used or reproduced in any manner whatsoever without written permission except in the case of brief quotations embodied in critical articles and reviews.

Library of Congress Control Number: 2022948674
ISBN (HB): 978-1-63655-072-5
ISBN (EBOOK): 978-1-63655-073-2

25 26 27 28 29 TLF 10 9 8 7 6 5 4 3 2

First Edition
Printed in China

RedCometPress.com

EXTINCTOPEDIA

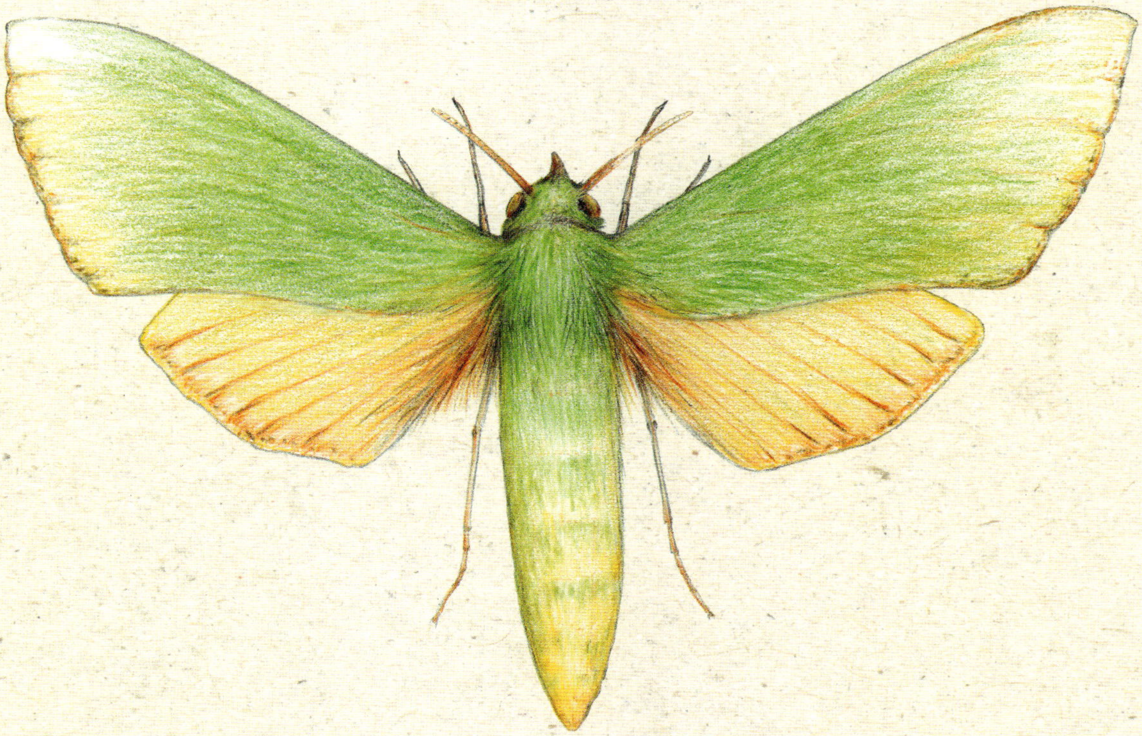

Written by
Serenella Quarello

Illustrated by
Alessio Alcini

Translated by Margaret Greenan

RED COMET PRESS · BROOKLYN

“Do we need wolves? Do we need to save animals? No, we do not. Just like we don’t need Mozart.”

What did Fulco Pratesi* mean by these words?

If the Earth were covered only by monoculture and intensive farming, we would not have the thousands of species (many in danger of extinction), that are essential for the health of our planet.

Maybe we could survive without wolves and Mozart, but we’d lose small yet significant forms of diversity and beauty along with them.

As with music, a beautiful painting, a funny video game, or an interesting book, even the rarest animal makes our planet richer, more diverse, and more beautiful. Each and every animal is necessary for the health of the planet, and if we lose them, it will change the planet as we know it forever.

We invite you on a journey to discover which animals are no longer with us, and which are at risk of disappearing. Find out what you can do, what we all can do, to save these precious forms of life.

*Fulco Pratesi is an Italian environmentalist, journalist, and politician who founded the Italian chapter of the World Wildlife Fund and currently serves as its president.

In the world, there are currently around 34,000 known species of fish, 8,100 amphibians, 10,400 reptiles, 10,900 birds, 6,500 mammals, and many millions of invertebrates, some one million of which are insects.

TWO HEARTBREAKING STORIES

MARTHA AND GEORGE

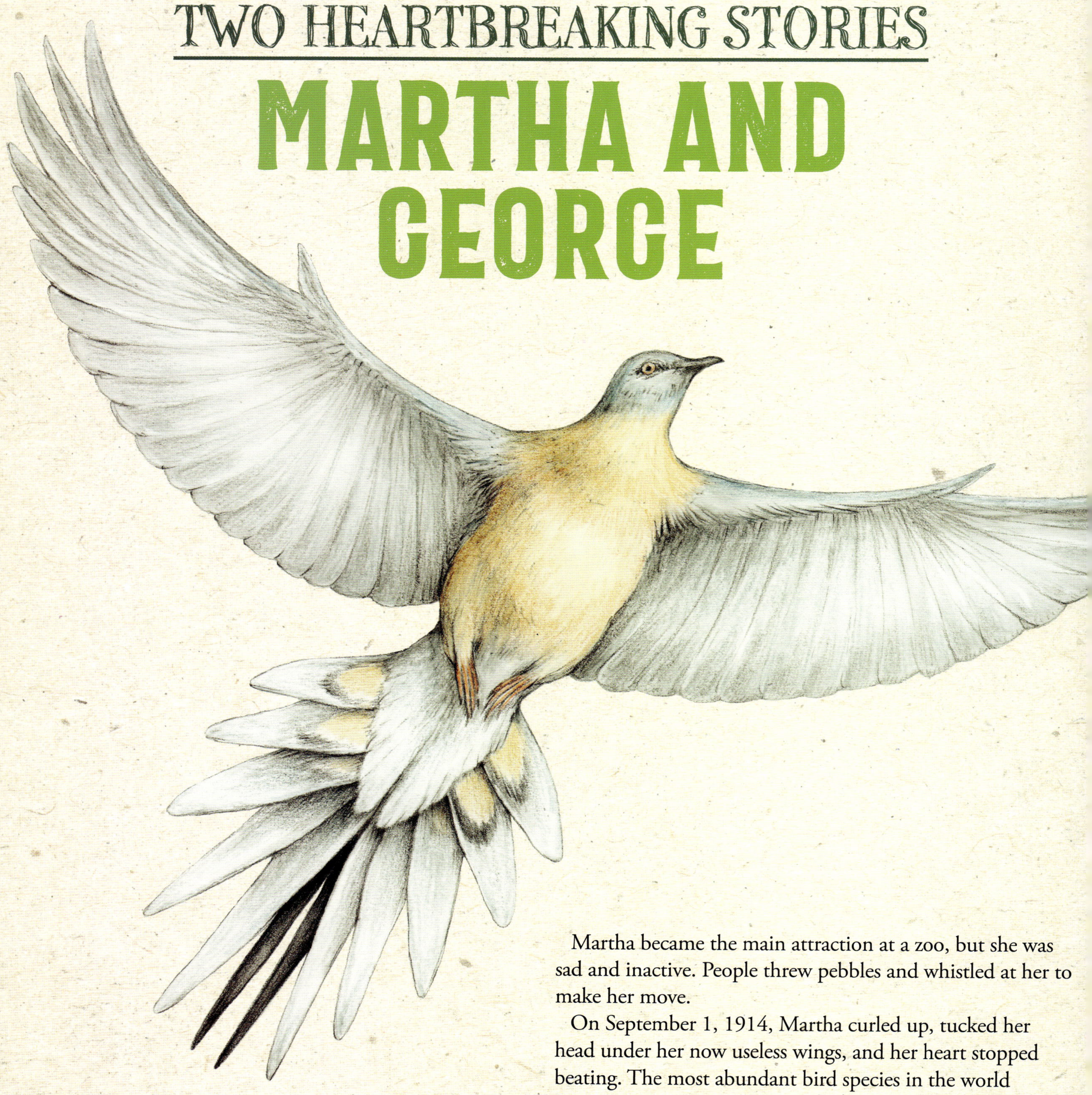

Martha, the last passenger pigeon

There was a time flocks of passenger pigeons were so huge they would make the sky dark. Then the big hunt began, and their bodies fell to the ground in piles; the hunters snatched as many as they could, and the rest were used as food for pigs or to fill holes in the roads. The trees in which they would lay their single precious egg were destroyed, and eventually there was only one bird left: Martha.

Martha became the main attraction at a zoo, but she was sad and inactive. People threw pebbles and whistled at her to make her move.

On September 1, 1914, Martha curled up, tucked her head under her now useless wings, and her heart stopped beating. The most abundant bird species in the world became officially extinct. Martha's body was frozen and sent to the Smithsonian Institution in Washington, D.C. People felt shame for what they had done, and for the failure of the Lacy Act of 1900, which was the first law enacted to protect bird species. Sadly it had not been enough to save Martha, the last of her kind.

The **passenger pigeon** (*Ectopistes migratorius*) was widespread in North America. It looked more like a dove than a pigeon. It was part of the Columbidae family, about 10 to 15 inches (30 to 40 cm) long, of gray-blue-brown color with a red chest. It fed on berries, fruit, and seeds.

Extinct animals

An animal is called extinct when there is no doubt that the last member of its species has died.

George, the loneliest snail in the world

Once, on Oahu Island in Hawaii, there lived a species of super snails called **yellow-tipped tree snails** (*Achatinella apexfulva*). They were endemic to Hawaii; endemic means they were native and found only in that specific area. These warriors had to fight against some terrible enemies: **rats** (*Rattus*) and the **rosy wolfsnail** (*Euglandina rosea*), a cannibal snail!

A team of zoologists saved a few specimens, putting them in a glass case. Many little snails were born there, including shy George; he didn't like coming out of his shell at night, and he never knew what it meant to slither freely in the undergrowth, evading enemies to scarf down some delicious putrefying leaves.

An epidemic hit the colony, exterminating all the snails except little George; as he was inside, he was protected from infection.

Snails are hermaphrodites, which means they have both masculine and feminine features (so the masculine name George is misleading). But they still need a mate to reproduce, so George died in 2019 without heirs. The beautiful shells of yellow-tipped tree snails, with their white, yellow, cream, and brown spirals, used to attract tourists who bought them as souvenirs. They didn't know that even a small snail was an important part of the entire ecosystem: they are useful decomposers, and they keep mold and algae under control in the wet undergrowth.

LOST FROM THE SKIES

FEATHERED FRIENDS THAT HAVE LEFT US

Cuban macaw

Who hasn't seen an image of the red and green or blue and yellow macaw on the shoulder of a pirate? The **Cuban macaw** (*Ara tricolor*) was caught for its meat even though it tasted bad, and it was captured as a pet, because of its harlequin-like colors, until it completely disappeared in the late 19th century.

Other extinct parrots are the parakeet of the Seychelles, **Newton's parakeet** (*Psittacula exsul*), the **Mascarene grey parakeet** (*Psittacula bensoni*) and the **broad-billed parrot** (*Lophopsittacus mauritianus*), both from Mauritius, and the **Jamaican red macaw** (*Ara gossei*).

North American heath hen

The **heath hen** (*Tympanuchus cupido cupido*), a type of pinnated grouse, so named in honor of its favorite heathland habitat, had "horns" made of pointed feathers. It is believed that in America it was the traditional dish for the first Thanksgiving. When people realized they were eating them all, they tried to save them, but it was too late. In 1932, this species (subspecies according to some) became extinct, but it led to the protection of other endangered birds.

Carolina parakeet

Due to its fondness for seeds and fruit, the **Carolina parakeet** (*Conuropsis carolinensis*) was considered a pest by farmers who culled them in large numbers. Its empathetic nature hastened its extinction, as once it heard a shot, it had to go back to see what had been killed. The Carolina parakeet became extinct in 1918, but was only officially declared so in 1939.

Huia

Measuring as long as 20 inches (50 cm), the **Huia** (*Heteralocha acutirostris*), so-called due to its *hu-ia hu-iaaaa* call, had an orange caruncle (a kind of callus), a long, curved beak for finding worms under the bark of trees, and beautiful glossy black plumage. Its tail feathers were used to decorate ladies' hats. The Māori people of New Zealand considered its quills a precious gift, which they kept in a *waka huia*, an inlaid jewelry box.

Labrador duck

Discovered on a spur of rock along the coast of Labrador (Canada) in 1789, the **Labrador duck** (*Camptorhynchus labradorius*) became extinct in 1875. Its most striking feature was the male's "wedding suit," a combination of black with milky white. Its extinction was mainly due to hunting, collecting feathers to stuff cushions, and changes to the coastal habitat where it lived.

STUDY THEM TO PRESERVE THEM

The precious remains of some extinct animals are kept in museums. It is important to keep studying them and looking into their DNA and the causes that brought them to extinction to protect similar species from the same fate.

Great auk

At 30 to 35 inches (75 to 85 cm) and weighing about 11 pounds (5 kg), this flightless bird resembled a penguin, but it was not. It was closer to a razorbill. The distinctive white band adjacent to its eye would get bigger or smaller depending on the season. It could be found on the shores of Spain, Canada, Greenland, and Norway. The last **great auk** (*Pinguinus impennis*) was sighted in 1852. It hid its eggs between rocks, but they would often be stolen by fishermen to make omelets. Some ancient Native American traditions also disappeared with the great auk, as it was considered a sacred totem animal. Today, it lives only in novels and in the popular video game *Assassin's Creed.*

Taxidermy

Taxidermy is a technique used to preserve an animal's skin with chemicals, and then fill it with a stuffing material to make it look alive.
In the past, animals were stuffed with straw or cotton, but nowadays foam models are used. Taxidermy should not be confused with embalming, which is a process of chemical preservation for an entire body.

South Island giant moa

The **South Island giant moa** (*Dinornis robustus*) is one of the nine species of giant "ostriches" that used to live in New Zealand. Unlike its distant relative, the common ostrich (*Struthio camelus*), the South Island giant moa was larger: 12 feet (3.6 m) tall and weighing in at 500 lbs (230 kg)! It had a long neck, powerful legs, and no wings, not even atrophied ones.

The Māori told legends about this giant ostrich. When they arrived on the island, the English didn't believe it had existed until a bone was found in the 1800s. It was sent to London, where Richard Owen studied it for four years until, finally, he was convinced: it was a real bone from a real bird that would not have been out of place in a horror movie! And so he named it *Dinornis* (*dino* = terrible and *ornis* = bird).

Moas feature sexual dimorphism: the female was taller and heavier than the male, just like the **kiwi** (*Apteryx australis*), the brownish bird that looks like the fruit of the same name. The kiwi is also from New Zealand and at risk of extinction.

WUNDERKAMMER

CABINET OF WONDERS

Wunderkammer, the ancestors of modern museums, were cabinets of curiosities, or "wonder rooms" (from German *wunder* = wonder, *kammer* = room), where scholars and nobles would accumulate collections to amaze their guests: silver-clad shells, carved corals, fake dragons and mermaids, stuffed animals, little monsters in formaldehyde, scary automatons, wax and chalk masks, ostrich eggs, narwhal tusks, mummies, and feather cloaks.

They appeared during the 16th and 17th centuries, a period of great geographic discovery. Once inside, it felt like the entire world had been squeezed in there. In the 1700s, people started to methodically classify, record, and preserve these collections, which were then opened to the public in the 1800s when museums first exhibited their contents for future generations.

In the 20th century, museums started having a "theme": science, antiquity, works of art, and so on. Today, they are also interactive sensory places where visitors can see, touch, smell, and experiment.

Stuffed animals under attack

The museum beetle (*Anthrenus museorum*), a small 0.01 inch (2 mm) bug, destroys stuffed animals by nesting between feathers, scales, and fur. Insecticide and larvae-proof cases are used to protect the animals, but it does not always work.

QUAGGA
(Equus quagga
quagga)
AUROCHS
(Bos taurus
primigenius)
BARBARY LION
(Panthera leo leo)

STELLER'S
SEA COW
(Hydrodamalis
gigas)
IRISH ELK
(Megaloceros
giganteus)
CASPIAN TIGER
(Panthera tigris
virgata)
CARIBBEAN
MONK SEAL
(Neomonachus
tropicalis)

MUSEUM ANIMALS

Caribbean monk seal

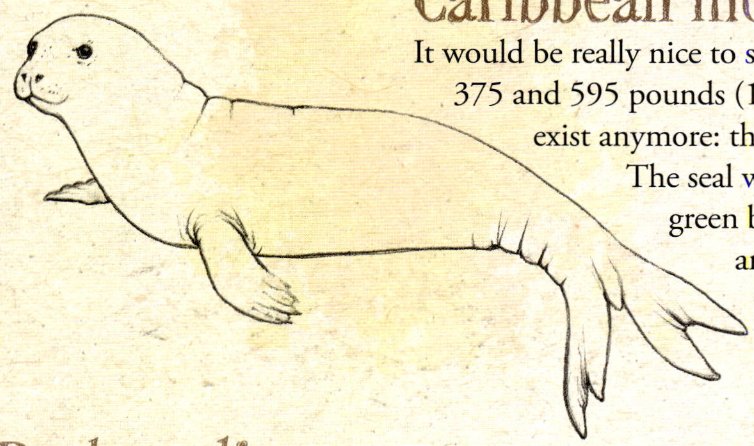

It would be really nice to see a **monk seal** (*Neomonachus tropicalis*) that weighs between 375 and 595 pounds (170 to 270 kg) and is 8 feet (2.5 m) long! Too bad it doesn't exist anymore: the last colony was spotted in 1952.

The seal was brownish grey (the color of a monk's robe), but it looked green because of the algae that grew in its fur. Its slowness, curiosity, and lack of fear of humans made it easy prey: Christopher Columbus wrote in his diary that he killed eight in one day to feed his crew.

Barbary lion

Morocco, 1942, Atlas Mountains. With the blast of a gun the majestic **Barbary lion** (*Panthera leo leo*), a 660-pound (300 kg) heavyweight of 11.4 feet (3.5 m) in length, falls to the ground, roaring for the last time.

Their manes were darker and thicker than those of savannah lions, to protect themselves from the mountains' cold. It was the biggest lion after the cave lion and the American lion. The Barbary lion was a symbol of strength.

Quagga

The **quagga** (*Equus quagga quagga*) took its name from its distinctive *kwa-ha-ha* call, and it was a zebra that looked a bit like a horse. Was its coat dark with light stripes or light with dark stripes? Scholar Reinhold Rau asserted it was a true optical illusion. They were hunted by Dutchmen and Afrikaners until the early 1800s. As a genetic relative of the Plains zebra, the quagga is considered an extinct subspecies. The Plains zebra is still very much alive today.

Aurochs

The **aurochs** (*Bos taurus primigenius*) is probably the ancestor of all the bulls, oxen, and cows in the world; it was a heavyweight of 1,760 to 2,200 pounds (800 to 1,000 kg) and roamed the plains of Europe, North Africa, and Asia.

It was so aggressive that killing one was deemed an act of courage up until the Middle Ages. Despite this, it was domesticated. The last of the aurochs, a female, died in Poland in 1627. Its skull is preserved in Stockholm's Royal Armory.

The bull that most resembles the aurochs is the Spanish Miura, which is bred for bull fighting.

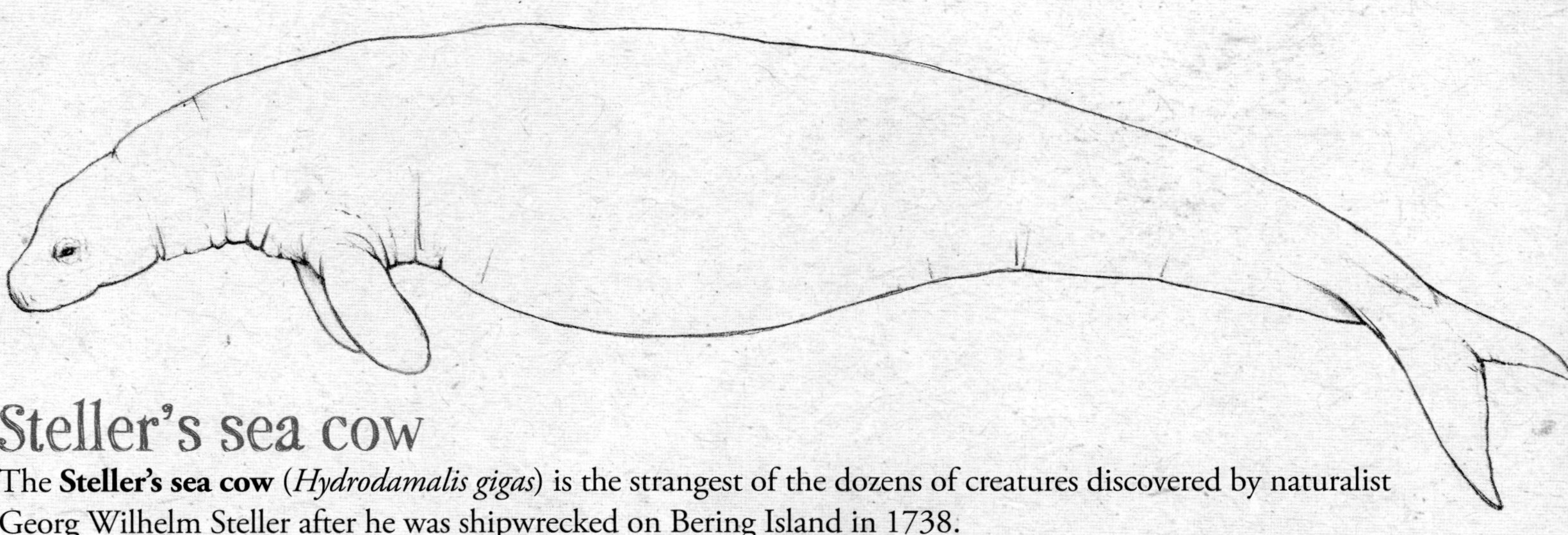

Steller's sea cow

The **Steller's sea cow** (*Hydrodamalis gigas*) is the strangest of the dozens of creatures discovered by naturalist Georg Wilhelm Steller after he was shipwrecked on Bering Island in 1738.

Imagine a giant seal-like creature with wrinkled skin. A relative of the dugong, it was a marine mammal, about 29 to 33 feet (8.8 to 10 m) long and weighing 22,000 pounds (10,000 kg); it loved sea "vegetables" so much it was nicknamed the "cabbage-eater."

While stuffing itself with seaweed, it was unaware of the seamen getting closer. They captured it as soon as it emerged to breathe. It became extinct just 27 years after its discovery.

Irish elk

The **Irish elk** (*Megaloceros giganteus*) was truly a "mega deer": its height at the shoulders was 6.5 feet (2 m), and its antlers could span 11 feet (3.3 m). It lived all over Eurasia between the Pleistocene and the Holocene epochs, so from 2.58 million years ago to about 9,000 years ago. But it wasn't actually an elk, nor Irish, even though many remains were found in Ireland, as it migrated to the British Isles when the sea levels went down at the end of the Ice Age. Prehistoric cave paintings tell us that it looked like a deer, with a little hump similar to a dromedary camel.

Caspian tiger

The **Caspian tiger** (*Panthera tigris virgata*) was 6.5 feet (2 m) long and its heaviest recorded weight was 529 pounds (240 kg). It was one of the biggest felines in the world, almost equal to the Bengal and Siberian tigers. It managed to survive until the 1970s, probably because it was good at hiding in the forests and long grasses, and lived along rivers in a range bordered by Eastern Turkey and Western China. Big hunting expeditions, the shrinking of its range (the geographic area where a species was distributed), and the horrible diseases that killed its prey, such as foot-and-mouth disease and swine flu, led to its extinction.

THE ALL-TIME CLASSIC

Dodo

The **dodo** (*Raphus cucullatus*), also known as "dronte," was a bird of the Columbiformes order, a relative of the dove. It was large and heavy—14 to 20 inches (35 to 50 cm) and 44 to 55 pounds (20 to 25 kg)—and native to the island of Mauritius. As it could comfortably live without migrating, its wings atrophied. In exchange, the dodo acquired a huge beak and two big legs it could use to search for the food that fell on the ground.

Its meat wasn't tasty (the Dutch used to call it *walgvogel* "disgusting bird"), and its feathers weren't used to decorate hats or helmets. How, then, did the dodo become extinct?

Imagine you're on the wonderful island of Mauritius—you're a dodo, hanging out with other birds like you: you're clumsy (*doudo* means silly in Portuguese) and have wings but cannot fly. You're distracted by juicy seeds, some deliciously rotten fruit, and *bam!* an arrow hits you and you end up roasted.

Moreover, the ship that brought the hunters was also full of cats, pigs, and dogs, which ransacked your eggs. Legend says it was the Portuguese and Dutch sailors who hunted it to extinction, but its annihilation was more likely caused by invasive species brought from abroad.

WANTED ALIVE

In 1983, American media mogul Ted Turner (founder of CNN) offered a $100,000 bounty to anyone who could catch a live thylacine. It was fruitless and the thylacine was officially declared extinct in 1986.

Thylacine

The thylacine, best known as **Tasmanian tiger** or **Tasmanian wolf** (*Thylacinus cynocephalus*), looked like a dog but was never domesticated. It was about 40 to 50 inches (1 to 1.3 m) long, 24 inches (60 cm) high, and weighed 45 to 55 pounds (20 to 25 kg). Like the Tasmanian devil, its closest relative, it had some powerful scent glands and would secrete a disgusting stench when agitated.

Only a few thylacines managed to live in captivity. They survived for 8 years at most and never reproduced.

The last one, Benjamin, died in Australia at the Hobart Zoo on September 7, 1936. September 7 has become Australia's national day for endangered species.

Four or five million years ago it was widespread across Australia and New Guinea, but 3,000 years ago its habitat shrank to just Tasmania. It was given its common name, **Tasmanian tiger**, because of the black stripes on its back, but it wasn't a feline; it was a marsupial. Like the kangaroo, it gave birth to underdeveloped young that would continue to grow in the mother's pouch, and it was quite common to see it bounce or stand up on its strong tail.

A legend of the Australian Aboriginal people explains that the black stripes on the thylacine's back are the result of some burns the animal got while trying to save the kangaroo, the bunyip, the great bird, and the platypus from a horrendous fire—an environmental catastrophe that unfortunately happens frequently in Australia, destroying acres of vegetation and the fauna that lives in it.

WHAT'S LEFT OF

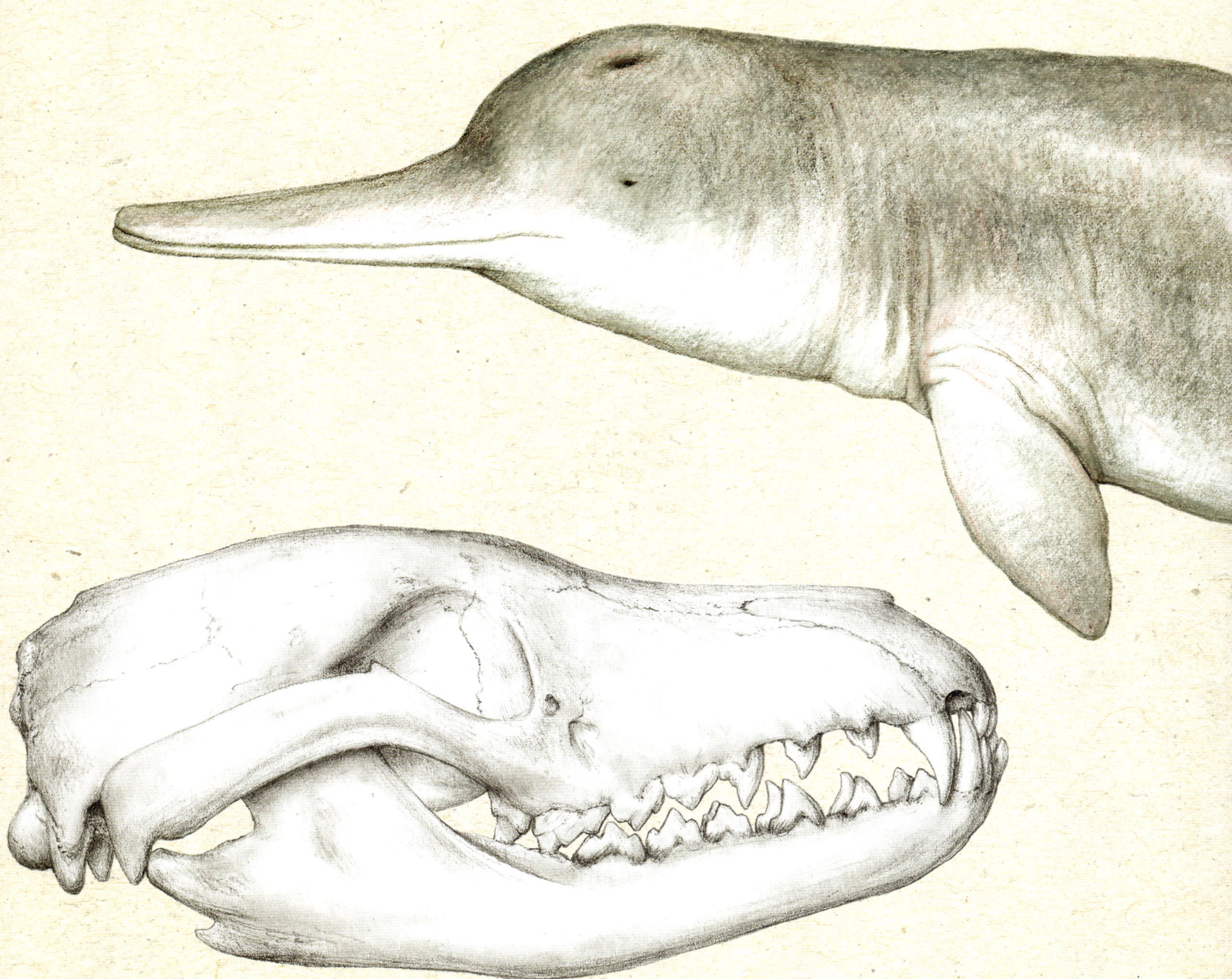

Thylacine

We have some remains of the thylacine's skin, skeletons, and skulls, which some professors at Oxford University use to test their students: some of these students fail their zoology exam because they mistake them for those of a dog or fox. We also have some black-and-white photos, like the one of farmer Wilf Batty looking full of pride next to the last thylacine killed in the wild in 1930.

With its barking and panting, the thylacine was easy to spot. As it was very shy, it scared easily.

In 2016, long after it had been declared extinct, the Booth Richardson Tiger Team was allegedly able to film one in a video shot by 24-hour camera traps. In 2018, a woman said she had seen two puppies in the Hartz Mountains in Tasmania. Anything is possible, but it's highly improbable.

THESE ANIMALS?

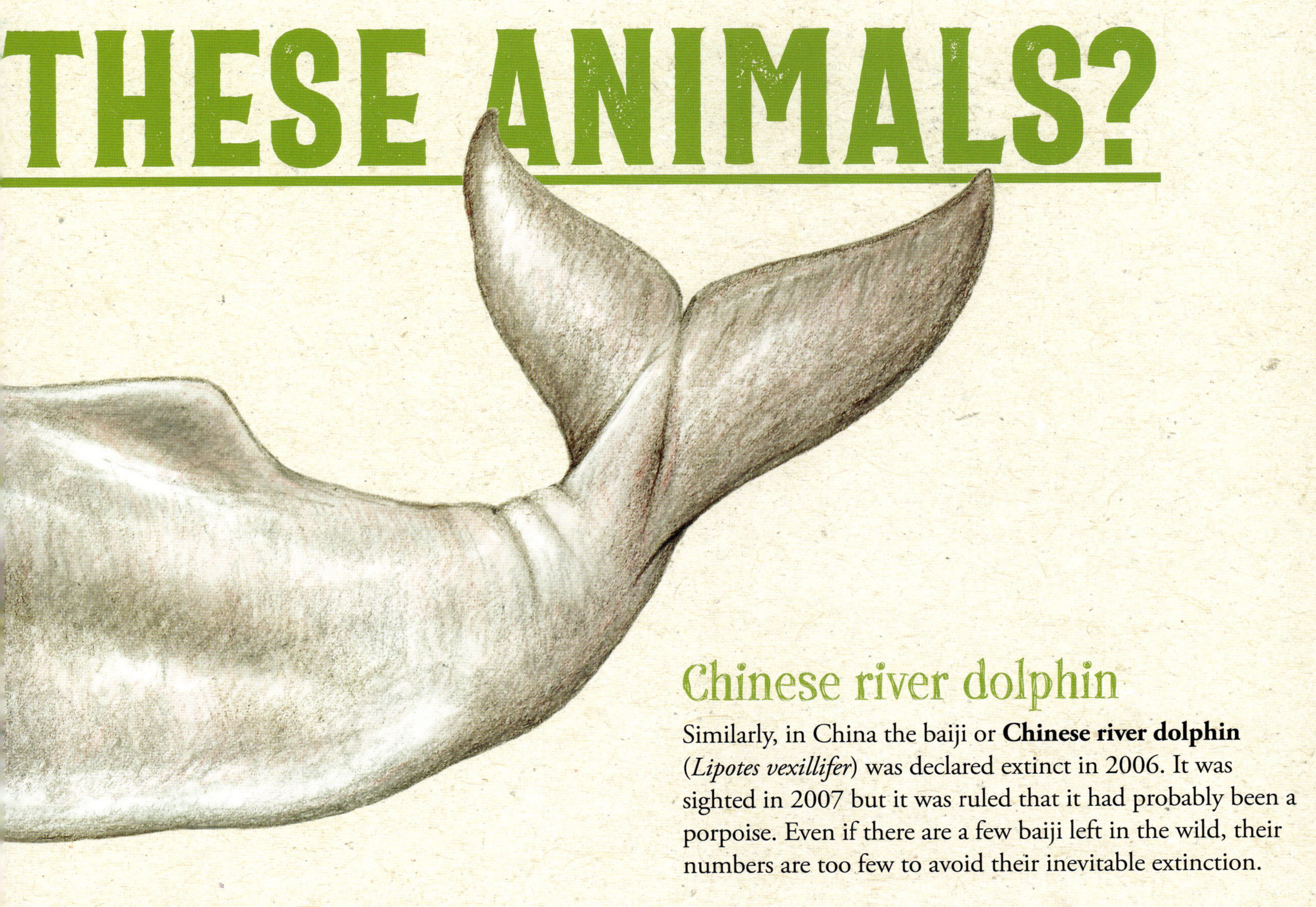

Chinese river dolphin

Similarly, in China the baiji or **Chinese river dolphin** (*Lipotes vexillifer*) was declared extinct in 2006. It was sighted in 2007 but it was ruled that it had probably been a porpoise. Even if there are a few baiji left in the wild, their numbers are too few to avoid their inevitable extinction.

Dodo

The last embalmed specimen of a **dodo,** preserved in the Oxford University Museum of Natural History, was thrown away because it had been gnawed on by moths. The only parts left are its head and a claw: Could they be enough to clone a new dodo?

This funny bird is still present in other ways, though: it can be seen in the Mauritius coat of arms and appears in many songs, movies, cartoons, video games, and novels. It is a brand of beverage, a jewel, a kind of car, and the symbol of an environmental organization. There's also a folk-pop-indie group: The Dodos.

MISSING...OR NOT?

DECLARED EXTINCT BUT REDISCOVERED

Starry night toad

The **starry night toad** (*Atelopus arsyecue*) was found 30 years after it was declared extinct thanks to some reports by the local native population in 2019. It is a black amphibian, 2 inches (5 cm) long, with white spots that made people say "Oh gosh, it looks like a starry sky!" when it was found. It probably survived in the Sierra Nevada de Santa Marta in Colombia. The inaccessible environment it lives in has protected it from its worst enemy: the fungus that causes chytridiomycosis. Of the 96 species of *Atelopus* amphibians, no fewer than 80 are endangered.

Bridled nail-tail wallaby

The **bridled nail-tail wallaby** (*Onychogalea fraenata*) is a marsupial. Its long name is due to the long white stripe that starts from its neck and surrounds its shoulders, and for the horny spur (actually a nail) on its tail. It is so fearful it freezes when it hears even a slight sound, hoping not to be seen!

It keeps its baby in its pouch for 4 months. Or should we say it kept? It was declared extinct until a fence manufacturer in the early 1970s saw a group of them on private property in Queensland, which has now been converted into a national park to protect the roughly 1,000 wallabies that live there.

Mountain pygmy possum

The **mountain pygmy possum** (*Burramys parvus*) is a tiny Australian marsupial with cinnamon-colored fur. It looks like a mix between a dormouse, a mouse, and an opossum. It feeds on pollen and nectar. It is a little guy that weighs 1 to 2 ounces (30 to 60 grams) and was believed to have been extinct since the Pleistocene era, but it was found in a ski town in 1966. Today, it is considered critically endangered.

Adelaide pygmy blue-tongue skink

The **Adelaide pygmy blue-tongue skink** (*Tiliqua adelaidensis*) is an Australian lizard. It had been declared extinct until one was found in the stomach of a snake in 1992. Bad luck for the lizard, but some really good luck for the researcher who found it before it was fully digested. This rare skink is no longer considered extinct but remains an endangered species.

Vietnam mouse-deer

Also known as the silver-backed chevrotain, the **Vietnam mouse-deer** (*Tragulus versicolor*) was believed to have disappeared for decades until it was "captured" in 2019 by about 2,000 shots of a camera trap in the undergrowth of a Vietnamese forest. It is a very special, even-toed ungulate (it has hooves) about the size of a rabbit.

LEGENDARY OR PAST LEGENDS?

The Quetzal, the bird-snake of the Maya

With its little yellow-green crest, its metallic-green head, and its bright red chest, the **quetzal** (*Pharomachrus mocinno*) is one of the most beautiful birds in the world. The feathers of its tail form a "train" that can be up to 39 inches (1 m) long!

To protect itself from predators, especially humans who desire its beautiful plumage, it hides among the everlasting fogs of the mountain cloud forests. Hidden between lianas, orchids, and parasitic plants, they swallow whole fruits, sit on branches, and wait 20 minutes for the pulp to come off the pit, which they then spit out.

It is easier to hear its sad, lamenting call (its nickname is *viuda*, "widow" in Spanish) than to see one. The Maya and Aztec people called it "sun bird." Its image—when combined with that of the snake—gave life to one of their strongest deities: the Quetzalcoatl or "feathered serpent." Its feathers were used to create some spectacular headdresses. The quetzal is also the name of the official currency of Guatemala; this beautiful bird appears on all its banknotes.

Today, the quetzal is a vulnerable species because of human deforestation to make room for coffee plantations.

The Harpy, Ulysses's ancient siren-eagle

The **harpy eagle** (*Harpia harpyja*) is one of the biggest and strongest raptors on our planet. It reaches 3.2 feet (1 m) long, has a 6.5-foot (2 m) wingspan, weighs 22 pounds (10 kg), and has powerful claws. It presents sexual dimorphism: the male is smaller than the female. The heaviest weight recorded was Jezebel, a 33-pound (15 kg) female that lived in captivity. Such a weight would be rare in the wild.

The harpy has a white belly, black wings, and striped tail and legs. Its pearl-grey head has a crest that lifts if someone is threatening it or its offspring.

In mythology, harpies were sirens with the body of a raptor and the head of a woman. They tried to charm Ulysses with their singing, but this didn't work because the Greek hero had himself tied to his ship's mast. Ancient Greeks also believed that harpies were like witches, and that they kidnapped children.

Native Americans also thought harpies were mythical creatures. They would search for nestlings, because those who were able to raise one were regarded as true chiefs.

Harpies build their nests on the highest trees of tropical forests between Mexico and northern Argentina. They dive from there, skillfully flying through lianas and branches to capture their prey (coatis, sloths, and snakes).

Harpies need a really big hunting area and are threatened by the deforestation of the rain forests, like so many other species.

THE REASONS FOR EXTINCTION

The case of the Irish elk*

During the Pleistocene era, forests were inhabited by megafauna, large animals whose numbers gradually reduced until they disappeared. This is what happened to this poor *Megaloceros* and its woolly friends: giant deer, giant elks, and mammoths.

When the Earth's surface changed, they moved onto islands and peninsulas, and their size became smaller over time. Is it possible that their big antlers and small bodies might have influenced their extinction? Running with 66-pound (30 kg) antlers on your head must be hard, right? This theory has been disproven by Stephen Jay Gould: their antlers were neither so big they got caught in branches, nor too small to attract females. Instead, what made Irish elks weaker was the scarcity of food caused by climate change.

Moreover, while past natives had been respectful and hunted only what they needed, the advent of great voyages starting in the 16th century saw seamen and hunters ruthlessly kill many animals, leading to their extinction.

* *See page 19*

Humans: the first culprits

The situation has gotten worse in the last 150 years. Some scholars estimate that, at the current rate, the number of extinct species could soon equal the extinction of dinosaurs.

On Earth, more than 2 million species of animals and plants have been cataloged by scientists, but there are currently many more to identify. Unfortunately, it is believed that about a million species are at risk and around 30,000 disappear every year.

TODAY

Deforestation

Cutting forests to make room for intensive farming. The impact is bigger on so-called "specialized" species, which can't tolerate changes very well.

Hunting

In the past, people hunted for food, to produce fur products, or to kill off animals that were considered harmful. Today, hunting is regulated by laws that are often not observed, and poaching (illegal hunting) is widespread in the world.

Colonization

As the human population gets bigger, the animal one gets smaller.

Pollution

Pesticides and chemical products get into the food chain of wild species. Industrial waste ends up in waterways. Plastic islands are floating in the oceans, with some plastics ending up in the stomach of marine species.

Skin Trade

Every year, 15 million wild animals are killed for their skins. Twenty four fox skins are needed to make one fur coat!

Eating

Many animals at risk of extinction end up on the table because they are deemed to be delicacies, like monkeys, pangolins, or the nests of swallows.

Collecting

Around 5,500 species of protected animals are illegally sold to private zoos, collectors, and circuses; a lot of them die on their journeys from places like Africa, Asia, or South America.

Treatments

Many animals are at risk of extinction because some people believe, without grounds, that some parts of their bodies have magical powers or can cure illnesses. Among them are the tiger and the rhinoceros, which are used in traditional Chinese medicine.

Fishing

Fishing with trawl nets catches a lot of different species, many of which aren't even edible.

Burning

Many fires are ignited by people or caused by global warming. Big wildfires, like the ones in Australia, destroy huge portions of land and reduce the number of animal species.

KEEPING TRACK OF ENDANGERED SPECIES

The superheroes of defense

The **IUCN** (**The International Union for Conservation of Nature,** iucn.org) is on the frontlines of defense and conservation of the environment, biodiversity, and animals—coordinating a global network of organizations from its headquarters in Switzerland.

The Red List

Each year, with the help of environmental organizations, experts, and volunteers from all around the world, the IUCN drafts the **Red List of Threatened Species**. The extinction risk of each animal is categorized as such: **EX** Extinct, **EW** Extinct in the wild, **CR** Critically endangered, **EN** Endangered, **VU** Vulnerable, **NT** Near threatened, **LC** Least concern, **DD** Data deficient, **NE** Not evaluated. More than 130,000 species have been evaluated for the Red List and the goal is to reach 160,000. Over 40,000 species are threatened. (They are in the CR, EN, VU, NT categories.) This is the most complete inventory of animal and plant species on the planet.

CITES: when exotic species end up on the market

The **CITES** (**Convention on International Trade in Endangered Species,** cites.org) was created in 1973 to keep a close watch on the international trade of wild species. Chameleons in handbags, shells and pangolins in suitcases, and monkeys hidden in trucks crossing borders are seen every day and the numbers are rising, even though the environmental police are very active and most governments forbid the importation of exotic species. More than half of these animals don't survive the journey.

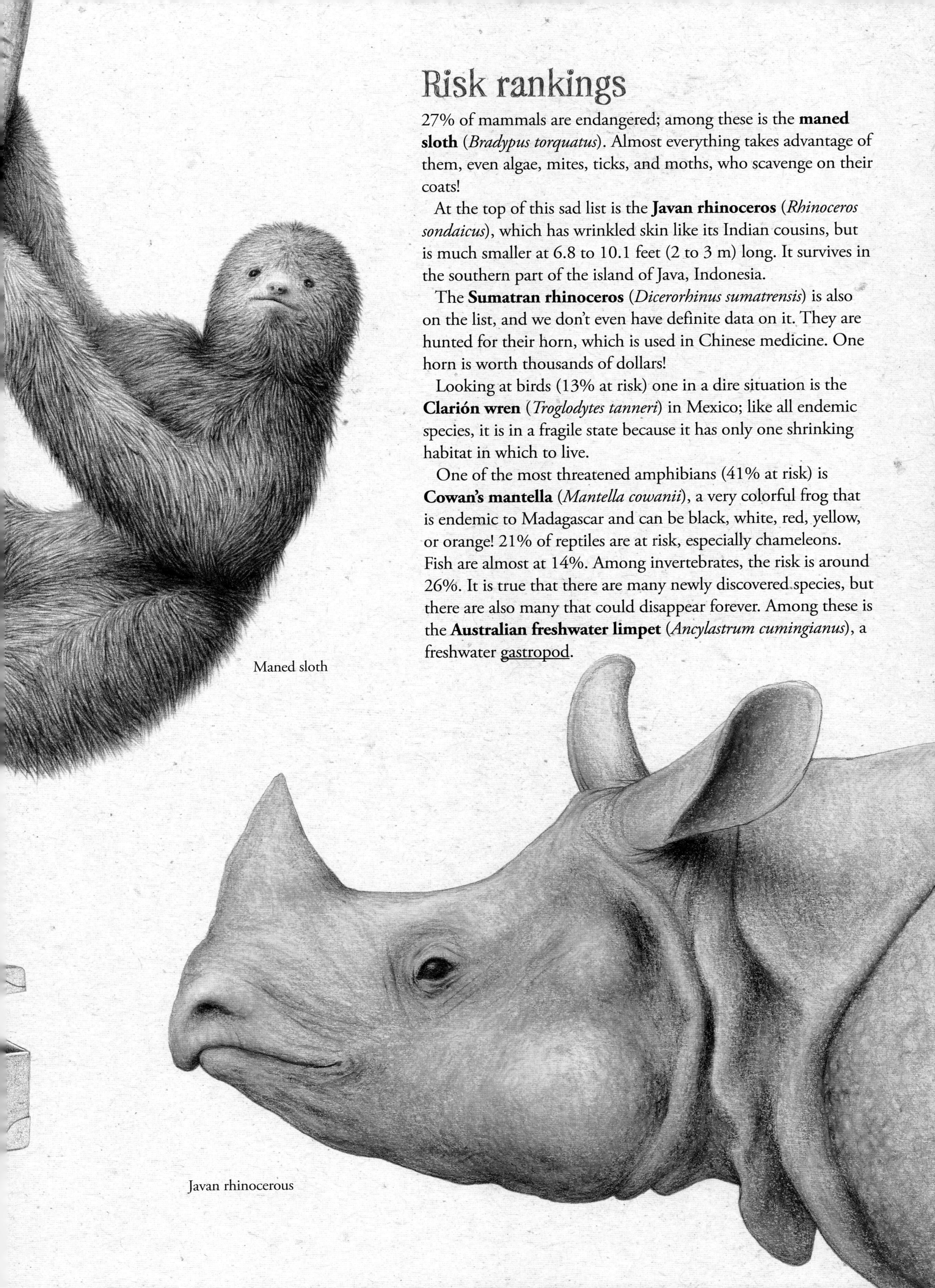

Risk rankings

27% of mammals are endangered; among these is the **maned sloth** (*Bradypus torquatus*). Almost everything takes advantage of them, even algae, mites, ticks, and moths, who scavenge on their coats!

At the top of this sad list is the **Javan rhinoceros** (*Rhinoceros sondaicus*), which has wrinkled skin like its Indian cousins, but is much smaller at 6.8 to 10.1 feet (2 to 3 m) long. It survives in the southern part of the island of Java, Indonesia.

The **Sumatran rhinoceros** (*Dicerorhinus sumatrensis*) is also on the list, and we don't even have definite data on it. They are hunted for their horn, which is used in Chinese medicine. One horn is worth thousands of dollars!

Looking at birds (13% at risk) one in a dire situation is the **Clarión wren** (*Troglodytes tanneri*) in Mexico; like all endemic species, it is in a fragile state because it has only one shrinking habitat in which to live.

One of the most threatened amphibians (41% at risk) is **Cowan's mantella** (*Mantella cowanii*), a very colorful frog that is endemic to Madagascar and can be black, white, red, yellow, or orange! 21% of reptiles are at risk, especially chameleons. Fish are almost at 14%. Among invertebrates, the risk is around 26%. It is true that there are many newly discovered species, but there are also many that could disappear forever. Among these is the **Australian freshwater limpet** (*Ancylastrum cumingianus*), a freshwater gastropod.

Maned sloth

Javan rhinocerous

WHO'S THE REAL ENEMY?

The wolf: the endless story

The **gray wolf** (*Canis lupus*) is present in North America and Eurasia. It can be up to 6 feet long (1.8 m) and 35 inches (90 cm) high and weighs between 79 and 108 pounds (35 to 50 kg); its coat ranges from gray to white (Arctic wolf), red (red wolf), and black (Canadian). Today, there are 14 subspecies, as well as similar species like the jackal and domestic dogs.

Wolves live in families made up of around 5 to 10 individuals. Men have hunted them since the Middle Ages. Shepherds see them as devourers of herds, hunters see them as competitors, and fairy tales have depicted them as child-eating monsters.

People tried to wipe them out with traps, guns, and poison. The wolf's diet includes mostly wild prey, but also fruit and vegetables. (They really like melons!) They don't mind refuse either, so they forage in urban places. Wolves are shy, and attacks against humans are almost nil.

Today, thanks to the creation of parks, conservation projects, and reintroduction programs (such as in the United States), and to the compensation given to farmers for the few sheep that are taken by wolves, they have started to repopulate many areas of the planet.

Despite still being hunted, poisoned, and hit by cars, the IUCN's Red List has classified the wolf as of "least concern."

Gray wolf

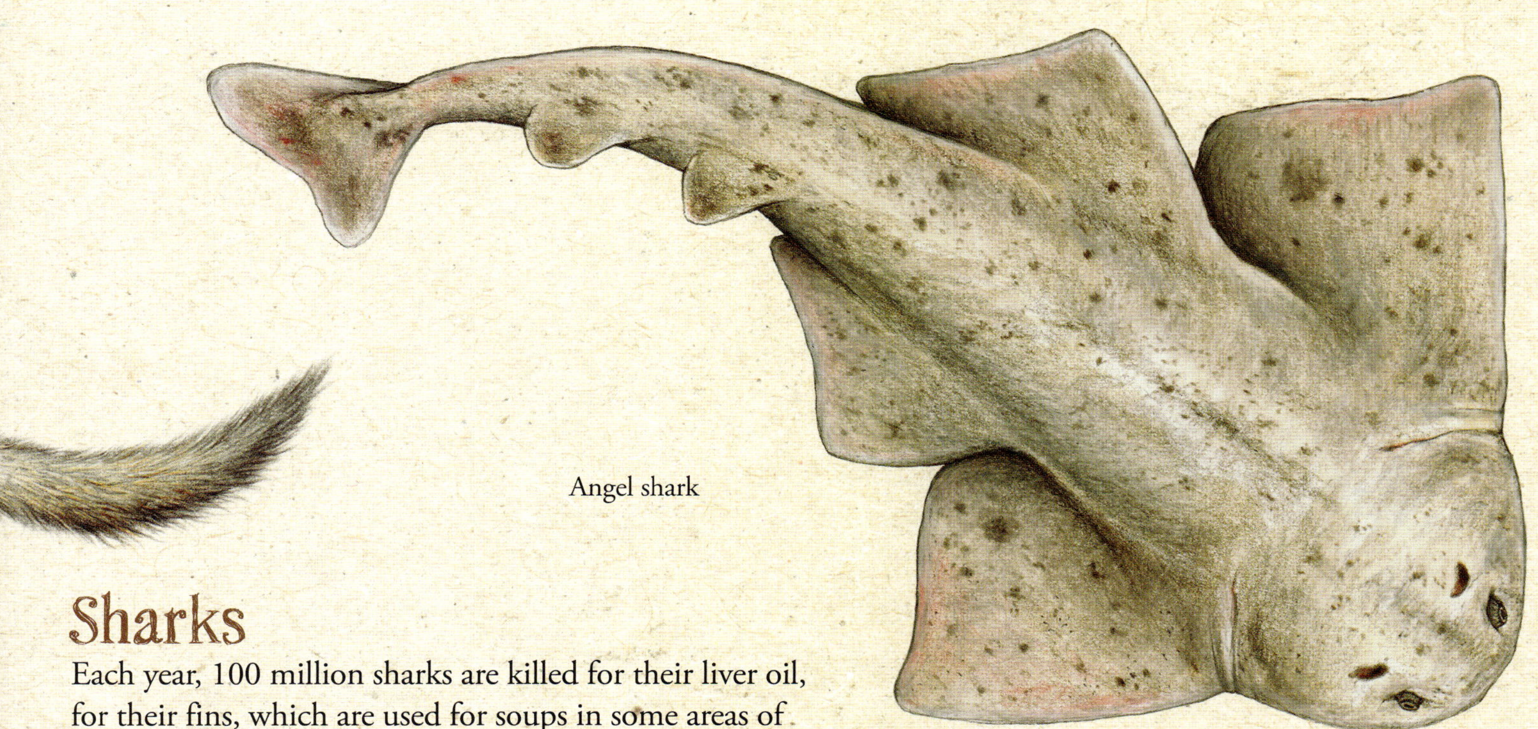
Angel shark

Sharks

Each year, 100 million sharks are killed for their liver oil, for their fins, which are used for soups in some areas of Asia, or for "sport."

A third of the world's 440 shark species are at risk of extinction, especially the **angel shark** (*Squatina squatina*) and the **daggernose shark** (*Isogomphodon oxyrhynchus*). Even the **great white shark** (*Carcharodon carcharias*) is highly vulnerable. Several Eastern countries have finally forbidden the fishing of the gentle giant, the **whale shark** (*Rhincodon typus*).

Brown bear

Bears

Brown bears (*Ursus arctos*) have been hunted since prehistoric times because they were accused of preying on cattle. But, despite being the biggest carnivore on Earth, they mainly feed on fruit, or even grass.

Since the 18th century, with the spread of human habitation, bears have had two alternatives: retreating to inaccessible places or going into more populated areas to feed on trash. Unfortunately, bears who enter human settlements are often put down as people think they might be dangerous.

A bear called Papillon became famous in Italy for being able to "escape" an amazing three times, and Amarena, a female, was often seen walking around a small town in Central Italy with her cubs.

These big plantigrades are sheltered in some protected areas, like Yellowstone Park in the US or Italy's Parco Nazionale d'Abruzzo, which is the refuge of the super-threatened **Marsican brown bear** (*Ursus arctos marsicanus*).

Polar bears (*Ursus maritimus*) are endangered by the melting of ice caps in the Arctic region. The disappearance of its habitat has also led to less prey, and this white giant is not reproducing as before. The skin beneath its white fur, like its nose, is actually black!

Other species of the Ursidae family at risk are: the **white-chested bear** (*Ursus thibetanus*), some subspecies of the **black bear** (*Ursus americanus*), the **sun bear** (*Helarctos malayanus*), the **sloth bear** (*Melursus ursinus*), the **spectacled bear** (*Tremarctos ornatus*), as well as the **giant panda** (*Ailuropoda melanoleuca*).

THE PANDA AND THE TIGER

Giant panda

The **giant panda** (*Ailuropoda melanoleuca*) is the symbol of endangered animals, so much so that naturalist Peter Scott drew it as the logo of the WWF (World Wildlife Fund), founded in 1961 for the protection of the environment.

Giant pandas were not known in Europe until 1869, when explorer Armand David sent the skin and skeleton of a panda to the Natural History Museum in Paris.

The first naturalist who studied giant pandas, Alphonse Milne-Edwards, put it into the Ursidae family. He then created a "special category," naming it *Ailuropoda melanoleuca*, where *melanoleuca* stands for "black and white" and *ailuropoda* for "cat paw." This refers to its special paw, equipped with an extra thumb that they use to hold bamboo branches.

The giant panda is officially part of the bear family, and what makes it vulnerable is the disappearance of bamboo forests, which are its only source of nourishment. It is really hard for them to reproduce in captivity. The biggest group of pandas survives in the Chinese reserve of Wolong, in the Sichuan region.

Giant panda

Tigers

Up until the 19th century, **tigers** (*Panthera tigris*) were widespread from Turkey to the Caspian Sea and throughout Asia, including Indonesia. In India, there were about 40,000 individuals at the beginning of the 20th century.

Today, about 3,000 individuals in 10 countries remain. This is partially due to the use of tiger parts in traditional medicine and the destruction of its habitat through deforestation and the spread of human settlements.

Hunting is still their number one enemy, and this is done both for its fur and by those who think they pose a danger to cattle.

The Maharaja of Surguja (in central India), boasted he had killed over one thousand tigers!

Bengal tiger

Bengal tiger

The most famous and widespread tiger today is the **Bengal tiger** (*Panthera tigris tigris*). But there are other subspecies, all gravely endangered: the **Siberian tiger** (*Panthera tigris altaica*), the biggest living feline, whose fur becomes light in winter; the small and robust **South China tiger** (*Panthera tigris amoyensis*); and the "tiny" **Sumatran tiger** (*Panthera tigris sumatrae*).

The **Javan** (*Panthera tigris sondaica*), **Bali** (*Panthera tigris balica*), and **Caspian tigers** (*Panthera tigris virgata*) are already extinct.

Maybe the **Indochinese tiger** (*Panthera tigris corbetti*) will be saved. It can be up to 10 feet (3 m) long, is a swift swimmer and jumper, and is so strong it can knock down a buffalo. Its scientific name comes from James Corbett, a British hunter who killed a huge number of animals before he mended his ways and became a conservationist.

AT RISK BECAUSE THEY'RE STRANGE

The aye-aye, Madagascar's elf

The **aye-aye** (*Daubentonia madagascariensis*) is an arboreal animal, like squirrels. Its tail is longer than its body, like dormice. And its front teeth keep growing throughout its life, like rodents. With its long ears, it looks like a bat, but it doesn't fly. What is it, then?

The aye-aye is a lemur, about 22 to 24 inches (55 to 60 cm) long, with black-brown coloring and a fair collar. It was discovered by German zoologist Bruno Schreiber in the 18th century, confirmed by English naturalist Sir Richard Owen in the 19th century, believed extinct, and then discovered again by French naturalist Petter in 1957.

Today it is endangered.

Due to its nocturnal lifestyle, monster-like eyes, and bony fingers, especially the middle one, which is quite long, the tribes of Madagascar considered it a dangerous little guy, one that's best left alone. The Sakalava tribe exterminated them because they believed they hunted humans, piercing their hearts as they slept. The most likely cause for its endangered status is the pollution of tree leaves and the destruction of the rain forests where it lives.

The aye-aye is the only extant species of its genus and family, the Daubentoniidae, while its bigger cousin, the **giant aye-aye** (*Daubentonia robusta*), is already extinct.

The aye-aye uses its middle finger as a skewer to pick up the bugs and fruit it feeds on, and its big eyes to move better at night. If you meet one, it will come close to sniff you; it is a curious, friendly animal.

The Axolotl, the eternal baby

The **axolotl** (*Ambystoma mexicanum*) looks like it came straight out of a cartoon, but it is a true amphibian: a paedomorphic Mexican salamander. Paedomorphic means it maintains its young, larval features even when it is an adult.

At larva stage, it is aquatic and does not need much food. But if it starts eating a lot of meat, its metamorphosis will begin and the axolotl becomes terrestrial and very hungry.

It can have a lifespan of up to 15 years and lives in the lakes around Mexico City. The axolotl's numbers have been greatly reduced by the shrinking size of its habitat, pollution, and attacks of human-introduced fish like perch and tilapia. It is 5 to 6 inches (12 to 15 cm) long, has a large, round head, small eyes that look like pearls, and gills that resemble coral. It maintains a state of constant motion to extract oxygen from the water. Axolotls are usually brown with golden dots, but they can also be found as albino (golden), axanthic (gray), melanoid (black with golden and olive dots), and leucistic (pale pink with black eyes and bright red gills). Its little face appears to be smiling and then *snap!* it quickly catches its prey in a second. Shellfish, insects, worms, little fish: they are all swallowed in one bite.

Axolotls can regenerate their paws, organs, and parts of their brains: an ingenious miracle that involves stem cells, which are much talked about nowadays as potentially useful for human medical research.

The pangolin, the armored mammal

The **pangolin** of the *Manis* genus looks really cute, even though ants surely disagree as it can eat 7 to 10 ounces (200 to 300 gms) a day thanks to its sticky tongue, which is as long as its body. Besides being the only mammal covered in almost 10,000 scales, it holds another record: it is the most smuggled of protected animals. When scared, it curls up in a ball, so hiding one in a suitcase is quite easy. Being a living tank doesn't help at all: it is toothless, peaceful, and at most is capable of curling around a person's arm and scratching it with its scales.

In 2015, Chinese customs found and confiscated almost 3,000 frozen remains of pangolins that were destined for the black market. Today, pangolins are classified as "at high risk." It lives in the tropical areas of Asia and sub-Saharan Africa. Its name comes from the Malaysian word *pang-goling*, which means "the one that curls up." Its eyes are small and it has poor eyesight, but to make up for it, the pangolin has a great sense of smell so it can find nests of ants and termites to dig up with its big nails. There are 8 species of pangolin, including the **giant pangolin** (*Smutsia gigantea*), which is almost 6.5 feet (2 m) long, weighs 77 pounds (35 kg), and lives in Central Africa.

UNUSUAL AND UNIQUE
ANIMALS TO SAVE

Aeolian wall lizard ♀

Lizards

At 10 inches (25 cm), this lizard is a small, gray insectivore that also enjoys plants. It lays clutches of 4 to 8 eggs. It is active in summer, spending its time on rocks andin the Mediterranean foliage. The **Aeolian wall lizard** (*Podarcis raffonei*) has been nominated a WWF "ambassador" for endangered species in Italy. This small lizard lives only in the Aeolian archipelago, in Sicily, and is threatened by the pollution caused by tourists and motorboats.

Even the smallest, seemingly insignificant, animal has an essential function within our environment. If it disappears, it will have a negative effect on the ecosystem. Each animal living on Earth is a treasure we must preserve and protect, including those that can look "nasty," "ugly," or "scary." Biodiversity is our planet's greatest wealth.

Salamanders and frogs

The presence of amphibians indicates a place is not polluted; pollution is one of the causes of the disappearance of toads, salamanders, and newts, two of which, the **Supramonte cave salamander** (*Speleomantes supramontis*) and the **Monte Albo cave salamander** (*Speleomantes flavus*), are barely resisting extinction in a tiny area of Sardinia.

♂ Aeolian wall lizard

Purple frog

Let's move from Sardinia's mountains to India's Western Ghats, to look for the now almost-impossible-to-find **purple frog** (*Nasikabatrachus sahyadrensis*): known for its round and mushy appearance, this amphibian could also come to a bad ending.

Bats

People believe that bats get caught in our hair and are friends with Dracula. But none of this is true: bats are very useful insectivores, which means they love eating insects, including harmful ones, like mosquitos. Of the 1,400 bat species in the world, around 50 are vulnerable, like the tiny **hog-nosed** or **bumblebee bat** (*Craseonycteris thonglongyai*): a .07-ounce (2 gms) mammal that hides in caves in Thailand and Myanmar.

The greatest impact is caused by limestone miners or tourists, who invade its habitat to see what is probably the smallest mammal in the world. From tiny to giant: the **golden-crowned flying fox** (*Acerodon jubatus*), a huge fruit-eating bat with an impressive 5.5-foot (1.7 m) wingspan, is also at risk due to deforestation.

Bumblebee bat

Snakes

They can be up to 26 feet (8 m) long and are able to crush even enormous prey. However, several species of pythons and boa—especially those living in the Antilles, like the **Puerto Rican boa** (*Chilabothrus inornatus*) and the **Jamaican boa** (*Chilabothrus subflavus*), might not be able to save their skins much longer. In fact, the former's skin is used to make shoes, bags, and belts, while the latter is sought-after in the exotic animal market and is preyed upon by mongooses and pigs that were introduced by humans.

The rarest snake in the world is the **Saint Lucia racer** (*Erythrolamprus ornatus*), which is harmless and measures less than 3 feet (1 m) long. Mongooses were introduced to the Caribbean island of Saint Lucia, the racer's only natural habitat, with the purpose of driving out the **golden lancehead** (*Bothrops insularis*), but the Saint Lucia racer also lost out.

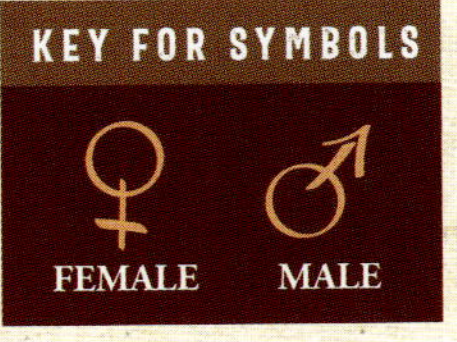

Saint Lucia racer

A - Syrian demoiselle (*Calopteryx syriaca*)
B - Wallace's giant bee (*Megachile pluto*)
C - European honey bee (*Apis mellifera*)
D - Crotch's bumblebee (*Bombus crotchii*)

E - Great diving beetle (*Graphoderus bilineatus*)
F - Dinosaur ant (*Nothomyrmecia macrops*)
G - Rosalia longicorn (*Rosalia alpina*)
H - Sabertooth longhorn beetle (*Macrodontia cervicornis*)

I - Apollo butterfly (*Parnassius apollo*)
J - Scarce swallowtail (*Iphiclides podalirius*)
K - Prairie sphinx moth (*Euproserpinus wiesti*)

AND WHAT ABOUT BUGS?

ANIMALS OF WONDER

"We'll be invaded by bugs. They'll be the kings of the world. They're the only ones resistant to pollution," people often say. But is it really true? Maybe it is for some kinds of invasive insects or those that are resilient, like beetles, flies, and stink bugs, but on a global scale, insects are disappearing eight times faster than vertebrates. It is estimated that almost half of them will soon end up on the IUCN's Red List of threatened invertebrates.

The **Apollo butterfly** (*Parnassius apollo*) has a sad history: it was the first to be taken into consideration by the Washington Convention (CITES) on the trade of endangered species. What were the causes? The usual: deforestation, loss of habitat, invasive species, climate change. Ants are also not safe, especially **dinosaur ants** (*Nothomyrmecia macrops*) and **red wood ants** (*Formica rufa*), skilled architects that are able to build giant nests made of pine needles and are tremendous warriors against harmful insects.

In the case of **honey bees** (*Apis mellifera*), aside from pesticides, their destruction is also caused by mites, viruses, bacteria, and fungi.

It is difficult to estimate how many **Homerus swallowtails** (*Papilio homerus*) are left in the wild, but it is common to see a large number of them pinned in the showcases of collectors, people willing to pay stratospheric prices to animal traders, despite the laws that regulate the collection of insects.

Monarch butterfly

Homerus swallowtail

This is worrying because Lepidoptera (the order of insects that includes butterflies and moths) tell us how the environment is doing: fewer butterflies = more pollution. The Homerus swallowtail is a huge butterfly with a wingspan of 5.5 inches (14 cm). It was once widespread across Jamaica, then its "family" was divided into small, isolated groups when its habitat, the tropical forest, was cut down to make way for managed forestry for wood production and palm oil.

The **monarch butterfly** (*Danaus plexippus*) is the most famous migratory insect. Why do millions of butterflies from Canada and the United States move south? The mystery was solved by Fred A. Urquhart, who "chased" them for 39 years by putting a bright tag on them. After some discussion between collectors, scientists, and students, an amateur entomologist found a hidden valley among some pine trees of the Michoacán region in Mexico. They were all spending winter there! For a long time, though, fir forests have been cut down to make wood, so this "queen" is at risk of disappearing. It needs a perfect temperature, high enough to prevent it from freezing but low enough for it to hibernate. It can only find that perfect temperature in this one specific area.

PLATANISTA, PORPOISES, AND CO.

The "dolphins" of sacred rivers

The **Ganges river dolphin** (*Platanista gangetica*) and the **Indus river dolphin** (*Platanista minor*) barely survive between India, Pakistan, and Bangladesh due to receding water levels and pollution. As more water is taken to irrigate crops and chemical fertilizers run off into the water, a deadly cycle is created.

Theses dolphins have pointed faces and sharp teeth; they're almost blind, but they are equipped with strong radar to hunt fish and prawns. Their dimorphism can be seen in the female's face, which continuously grows.

It is calculated that there are about 1,000 left today, but a sheltered area between two dams in Pakistan has recently celebrated the birth of some baby platanista.

Boto

The boto, pink Amazon river dolphin

The **boto** or **Amazon river dolphin** (*Inia geoffrensis*) is usually grey-white, but the skin of some individuals appears pink because their blood vessels can be seen through their skin. It lives in South American rivers but has also been spotted in flooded forests during the rainy season.

Its forehead has a little lump that can expand and protrude at will. Some indigenous people of the Amazon River believed the boto was sacred, and a legend says that the pink dolphin is actually a boy who wears a hat on his head during the day to hide his blowhole and then transforms back into a dolphin at night.

The boto's brain capacity is 40% bigger than ours and poachers take advantage of their sociable nature to hunt them.

Lagoon reserves have been created to protect them and have given good results, especially in Peru, but these dolphins are unable to reproduce in captivity.

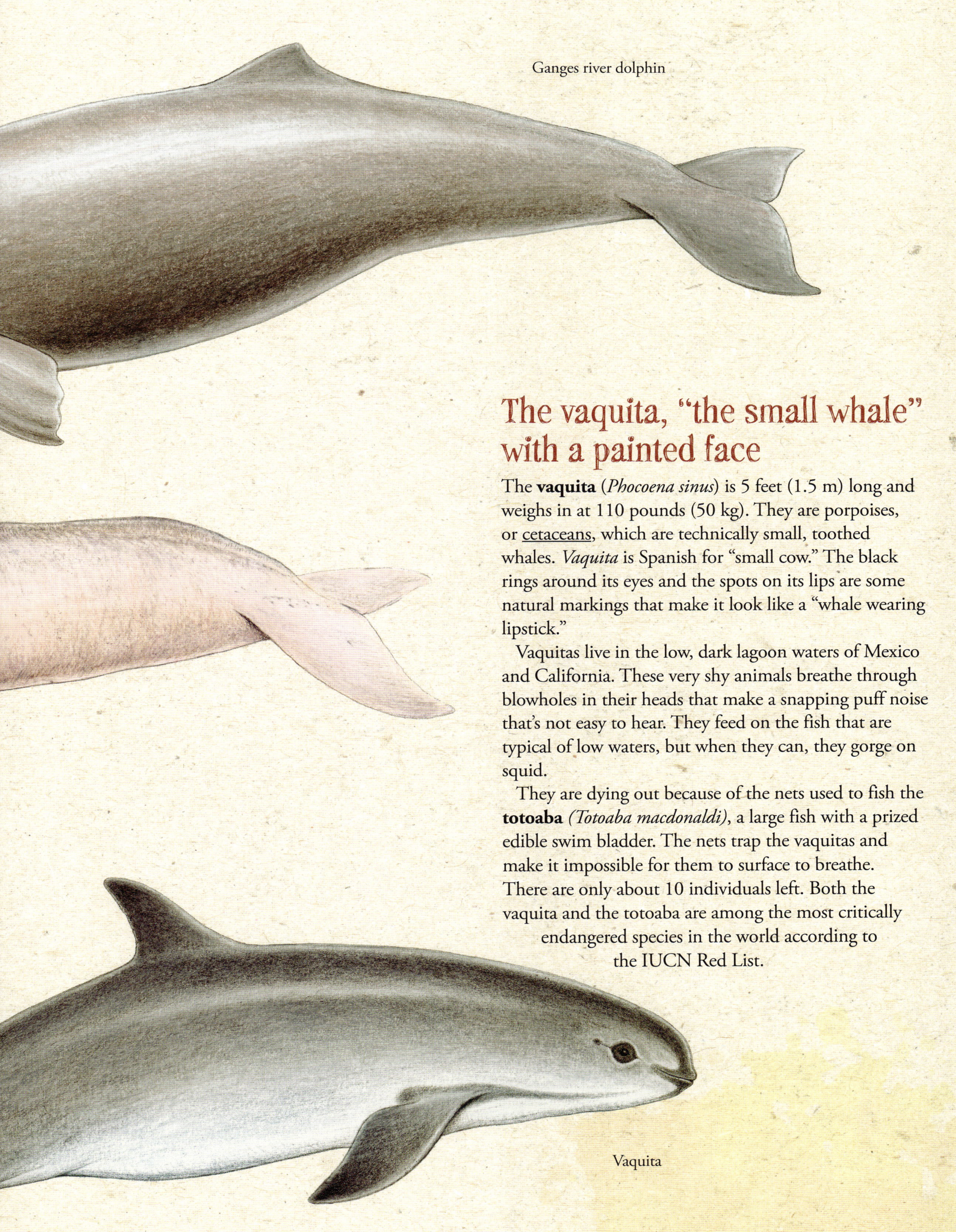
Ganges river dolphin

The vaquita, "the small whale" with a painted face

The **vaquita** (*Phocoena sinus*) is 5 feet (1.5 m) long and weighs in at 110 pounds (50 kg). They are porpoises, or <u>cetaceans</u>, which are technically small, toothed whales. *Vaquita* is Spanish for "small cow." The black rings around its eyes and the spots on its lips are some natural markings that make it look like a "whale wearing lipstick."

Vaquitas live in the low, dark lagoon waters of Mexico and California. These very shy animals breathe through blowholes in their heads that make a snapping puff noise that's not easy to hear. They feed on the fish that are typical of low waters, but when they can, they gorge on squid.

They are dying out because of the nets used to fish the **totoaba** *(Totoaba macdonaldi)*, a large fish with a prized edible swim bladder. The nets trap the vaquitas and make it impossible for them to surface to breathe. There are only about 10 individuals left. Both the vaquita and the totoaba are among the most critically endangered species in the world according to the IUCN Red List.

Vaquita

BIG MARINE MAMMALS

BIG PROBLEMS

When fishing is indiscriminate it spares no one: from common cod to krill, tiny shrimp that are the main food of whales. Krill are now fished to make feed for the livestock of intensive farms, which are one of the planet's main polluters.

Millions of tons of harmful substances and industrial waste are dumped into the sea: huge plastic islands are popping up everywhere, while coral atolls disappear forever.

Monk seals

Mediterranean monk seals (*Monachus monachus*) were already known to Homer who, in the *Odyssey*, described them as "numerous, lying on the beach and . . . stinking of sea a little." There were many, from the Mediterranean to the Black Sea, but the hunt was ruthless. Today, they are protected; even though there are more of them, proven by several sightings, their number is still worrying because of intensive fishing, nets, and accidents with motorboats. The few individuals left hide on the isolated beaches and caves of Greece, Turkey, and Croatia, and there are also some in Italy, where they are called sea oxen.

Coral

Coral, part of the class Anthozoa, are a colony of little polyps that "build" a structure made of calcium carbonate to support and protect themselves. Over time they form islands (atolls) or barriers like the famous Great Barrier Reef in Australia. Due to the global rise in water temperatures, 33% of coral reefs are at risk of extinction. As temperatures rise, the symbiosis between the polyps and the zooxanthella, a micro algae which feeds the coral through photosynthesis, is disrupted. A 2-degree rise is enough to starve the coral of the nutrients it needs.

Giants in danger

Whales have been hunted since 6,000 BCE to obtain oil and fat. Whaling ships used harpoons in the past, today they use explosives. A 1986 law allows whale hunting only for the local populations who cull them for food, but many countries keep killing them for commercial purposes.

Things look better for sperm whales, even though they are still hunted to obtain a precious substance, ambergris, used to make perfumes.

The **West Indian manatee** (*Trichechus manatus*), together with the **Amazon** (*Trichechus inunguis*) and **African manatees** (*Trichechus senegalensis*), is part of the Sirenia, an order of slow, meek, and herbivorous sea mammals. Commonly called sea cows, they are not related to cows. Can you imagine a cow that is over 10 feet (3 m) long, with hooves that were transformed into fins by evolution? They're easy to catch, edible, only reproduce every two years, and often get stuck in nylon nets. In ancient times people believed they were mermaids or sea monsters.

SHELLS AT RISK
AND ALIEN INVASIONS

Loggerhead sea turtle

The descendants of the big reptiles that lived in the Mesozoic era have maintained some of the features of their prehistoric ancestors: a hydrodynamic shape (for speed), sturdy fins, large, flat, propeller-like back legs (for propulsion), a head with a retractable beak, and a carapace (a strong shell).

Female turtles live on their own; they only meet up to build their nests on the beach. Then they dive back into the water, where their eggs are fertilized by males for their second brood. Many eggs won't hatch, others will be looted, and the little turtles will have to reach the water from their soggy shell before the sea birds raid them.

Turtles are threatened with extinction due to a variety of reasons including the use of their shells to make frames for reading glasses, ornaments, and fans. They get caught in fishing nets and eat plastic waste that they mistake for a favorite food, jellyfish. They are also consumed by humans in turtle soup. All these things risk the survival of these gentle creatures that have survived for 70 million years.

In the IUCN's Red List we can find: the **loggerhead sea turtle** (*Caretta caretta*), the **green turtle** (*Chelonia mydas*), the **hawksbill** (*Eretmochelys imbricata*), **Kemp's ridley** *(Lepidochelys kempii),* the **olive ridley** *(Lepidochelys olivacea)*. It's no better for the **leatherback sea turtle** (*Dermochelys coriacea*), a giant that can be up to 6.5 feet (2 m) long.

Leatherback sea turtle

Threats often come from so-called "alien species," those introduced by humans, which drive away or destroy the native ones. This is what happened to the **Galapagos tortoise** (*Geochelone elephantopus*), which is now under "special protection" as the fragile balance of its habitat has been under serious threat since the arrival of invasive species like dogs, cats, rats, goats, and humans!

In Europe, **slider turtles** (*Trachemys scripta*) from America were often sold as pets, but they grow big and are hard to keep at home, biting anything that appears in their tank, including fingers. They have been abandoned in rivers and ponds, where they are killing off the weaker species such as the **European pond turtles** (*Emys orbicularis*).

American slider turtle

European pond turtle

There are a lot of projects for the protection of sea turtles, including turtle hospitals and capturing them for preservation in captivity. But turtles are less likely to reproduce in an aquarium.

Among the strangest and most threatened are some Australian species like the **Mary River turtle** (*Elusor macrurus*), which is called "punk turtle" after the green tuft of seaweed that grows on its head, and the **pig-nosed turtle** (*Carettochelys insculpta*), which has a snout it uses to take in air while the rest of its body is submerged.

Pig-nosed turtle

OCEANIA

KOALA AND FRIENDS

Australia boasts some extraordinary fauna. It's the only place where we can find the **platypus** (*Ornithorhynchus anatinus*), a mammal that lays eggs, or the **green and golden bell frog** (*Ranoidea aurea*), which roars like a motorbike when it fights. It is so vulnerable that some sports fields designed for the Sydney Olympics were moved to avoid destroying its habitat.

Koala

Unfortunately, huge bushfires—which are caused by climate change and can last for several months—have devastated acres of the koala's range. When eucalyptus trees burn, **koalas** (*Phascolarctos cinereus*) suffer the consequences. They are part of the genus *Phascolarctos*, which translates as "pouched bear." They are marsupial climbers, hunted almost to extinction for their soft fur, which smells like eucalyptus, their main source of food.

Wombat

Another endangered marsupial species is the **Northern hairy-nosed wombat** (*Lasiorhinus krefftii*). During the big fires that devastate Australia, wombats act like heroes by allowing other species to save themselves in their burrows. But if a predator gets in, the wombat "knocks it out" with its butt. The "bricks" it uses to close up the burrow are its own droppings, which, thanks to its special bowels, come out as handy little cubes.

Kākāpō

The **kākāpō** (*Strigops habroptilus*), a big, sturdy parrot, is a one-of-a-kind nocturnal bird that lays its eggs on the ground. It is threatened by pigs, goats, and rats, but also by viruses, bacteria, and microscopic fungi.

Numbat

The **numbat** or **striped termite eater** (*Myrmecobius fasciatus*) is another super-protected marsupial that inhabits eucalyptus forests. At 14 to 18 inches (35 to 45 cm) long, it comes in various colors, but it always has two distinctive black stripes across its eyes and ears. It can wolf down 20,000 termites a day!

Bilby

If time is up for the extinct **lesser bilby** (*Macrotis leucura*), the **greater bilby** (*Macrotis lagotis*) could still make it. But what is a bilby or a bandicoot? We could say it looks like a cross between a mouse, a hare, and rabbit, with long ears and a long tail. It lives in burrows and digs in dry areas, but it is threatened by feral cats.

SCIENTISTS, STUDIES, AND SOME DISASTERS

The Lazarus Project

The **gastric-brooding frog** (*Rheobatrachus vitellinus* and *Rheobatrachus silus*) became extinct in the 1980s. It had a peculiar habit: once fertilized by the male, the eggs were swallowed by the female. After a few weeks, the froglets would pop out of its open mouth! Scientists in Melbourne have tried to put genes from this frog into the eggs of other Australian frogs, but it's a very difficult process.

Scientists have calculated that between 1,600 and 3 million species could disappear by the end of the 21st century: this data proves that the planet is unwell.

In the course of evolution, it is normal for some species to disappear; extinction it is a natural process. During Earth's history, there have been several mass extinction events from natural causes.

But when species disappear due to human activity; when the causes are deforestation, hunting, animal trade, climate change, and pollution, what can we do? What must we do?

Is it right to bring back to life an animal that we caused to become extinct?

These are the questions scientists ask themselves. Would you like to see saber-toothed tigers and dodos again? Scientists are trying to clone them. These attempts are called "de-extinction."

Celia's story

Celia was the last specimen of the **Pyrenean ibex** (*Capra pyrenaica pyrenaica*), an elegant ibex that is called *bucardo* in Spanish. A radio collar was put on her to track her movements, but a few months later the signal stopped: Celia was dead, crushed by a tree. A team of Spanish scientists tried to put some of her cells into goat eggs, and in 2003, a goat gave birth to a little clone of Celia; unfortunately, it only lived for a few minutes.

LOST AND FOUND DNA

The Russian Jurassic Park

Up until about 12,000 years ago, **mammoths** (*Mammuthus primigenius*) lived in Siberia and kept the land fertile with their manure. When they disappeared, everything became covered in moss.

A Russian ecologist decided to repopulate the area with **musk oxen** (*Ovibos moschatus*) and **horses** (*Equus caballus*), calling it "Pleistocene Park."

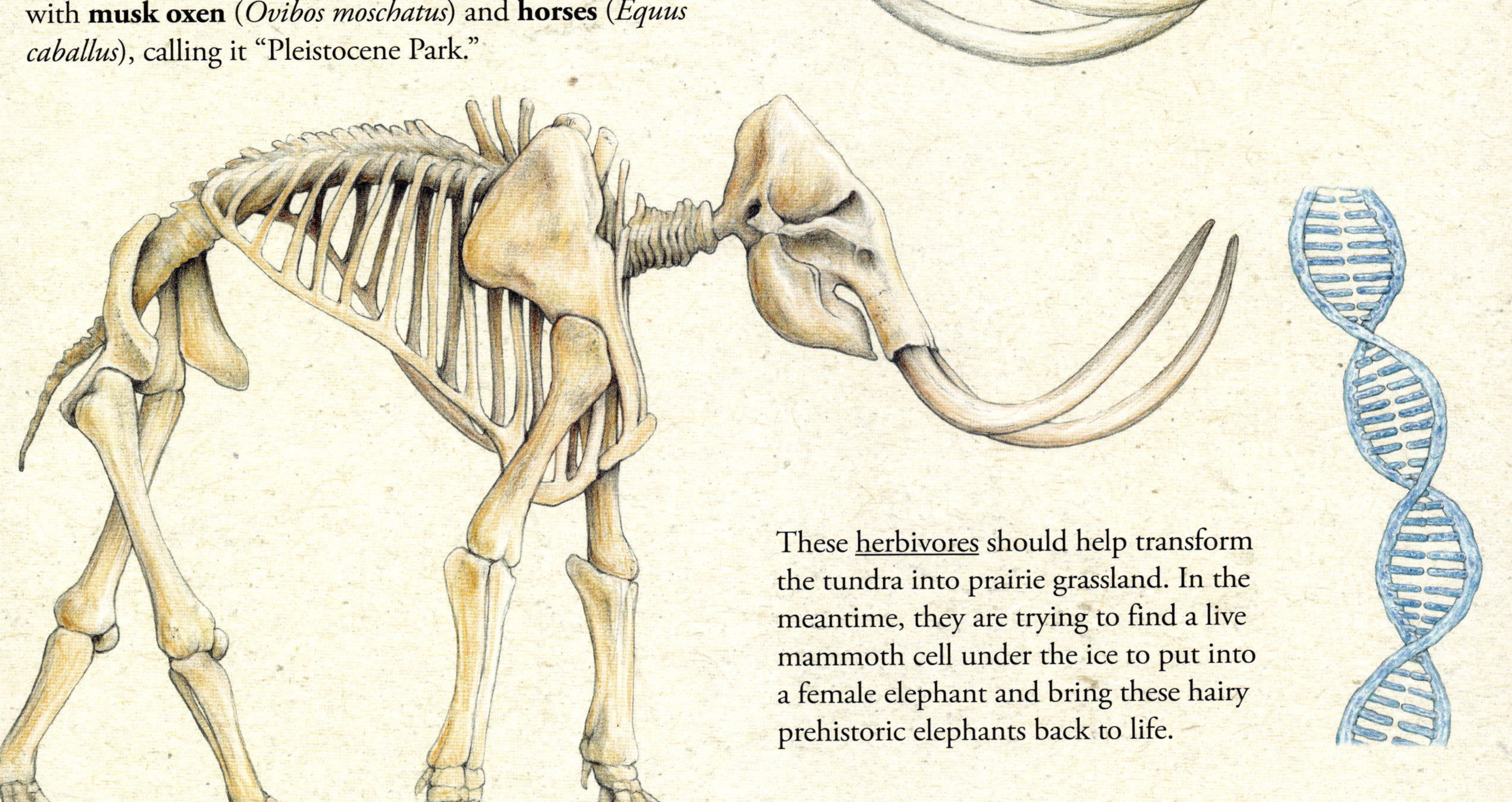

These herbivores should help transform the tundra into prairie grassland. In the meantime, they are trying to find a live mammoth cell under the ice to put into a female elephant and bring these hairy prehistoric elephants back to life.

Martha's story

An American scientist has discovered how to obtain and put together some pieces of DNA taken from the stuffed body of Martha, the last **passenger pigeon**.*

He is trying to collect cells of this extinct animal to put into a pigeon's egg. If a chick with a long tail and Martha's colors were to hatch from it, would it really be a passenger pigeon?

We don't know if it's possible and right to bring back the dodo, the moa, and all the other extinct animals, but we know it's right to do everything we can to protect the environment and the species that still populate the Earth.

*See page 8

ANIMAL PROTECTION

WHAT WE CAN DO

Great apes

"Our love for animals is measured by the sacrifices we are willing to make for them" is a quote by the famous ethologist (a scientist who studies animal behavior in the natural environment) Konrad Lorenz. This was especially true for scholars such as Jane Goodall, friend of the **chimpanzee** (*Pan troglodytes*), and Dian Fossey who spent her life studying **mountain gorillas** (*Gorilla beringei beringei*), showing that they were not as dangerous and aggressive as people believed. Their sacrifice has not been in vain: there are, in fact, several organizations, volunteers, and scientists who are fighting to save anthropoid apes, those closely related to humans, which have always been violently hunted despite the fact their DNA and ours is nearly the same.

Have you ever seen the sad face of an **orangutan** (*Pongo pygmaeus*) locked in a cage? They might be dreaming about the tall trees of the Indonesian jungle.

A particularly cruel method is used to capture the orangutan: the mother is killed to kidnap the baby. The mother orangutan is very doting: she stays with her baby for a whole four years and, to make sure it doesn't fall, uses herself as a bridge from branch to branch.

Have you ever heard **gibbons** (*Hylobatidae*) singing? It's the method males use to communicate without coming to blows. The females do vocal exercises like an opera singer, before having fruit for breakfast and throwing themselves from one branch to another with their long, prehensile arms.

Orangutans, gorillas, chimpanzees, and gibbons are so rare that, even though many are against them, parks and sanctuaries for rehabilitation are still the only way to save them. These reserves protect the last forests, teach the local population to respect them, and promote a more responsible kind of tourism.

A - triton snail
B - queen conch
C - giant clam

Shells and ivory

Ivory is obtained from killing **elephants, hippos, walruses**, and **narwhals**. Although it is forbidden in many countries and by CITES, every year several tons are confiscated and destroyed.

Besides turtles, the shells of mollusks are also in danger; such is the case of the **queen conch** (*Aliger gigas*), the huge **giant clam** (*Tridacna gigas*), once used as holy water fonts, and **triton snails** (*Charonia*), which were used as trumpets by the Romans and are one of coral's biggest allies against their main enemy: the **crown-of-thorns starfish** (*Acanthaster planci*).

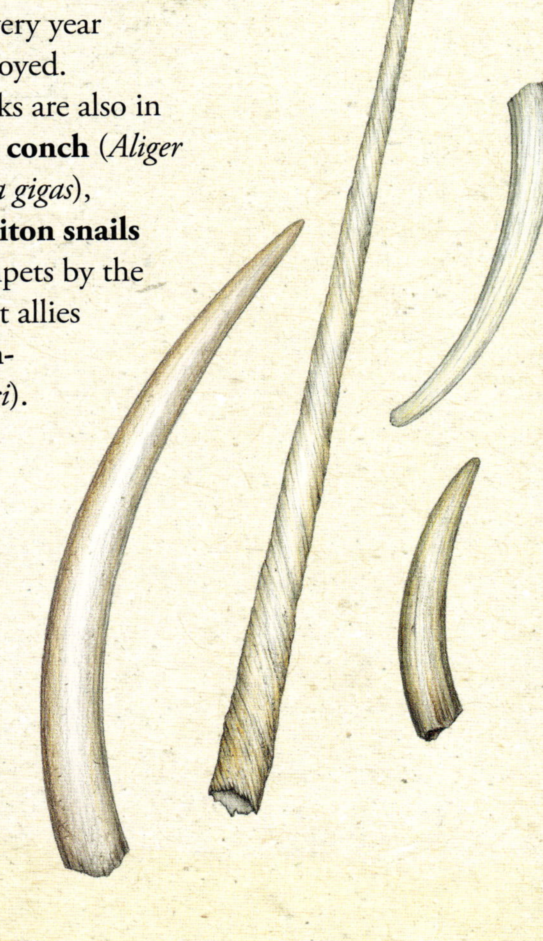

Examples of animal ivory

Get involved. You too can protect, defend, and help animals in difficulty.

If you like the circus, choose one without animals. Behind the tricks, the animals endure months of hard training and often cruel treatment; moreover, they are kept in small cages, without the company of other animals of their own kind, and forced to behave in ways they never would in the wild. Choose animal parks and centers that were created for the reproduction, study, and protection of endangered species and other animals.

Don't buy items made of turtle shells, shark teeth, seashells, starfish, or seahorses.

Support the organizations that are committed to animal protection and call a local veterinarian if you find an animal in need: they will tell you where you can find shelters that take care of wounded wildlife.

Don't buy exotic animals that come through illegal trade. It is your right to ask for the CITES certificate. Make sure that they're specifically bred as pets.

Every year, thousands of animals are caught by snares, traps, and nets, especially small birds and mammals. If you see a trap while walking in the wild, call the authorities. There are special departments for the defense of animals.

And keep studying . . . to learn more about them!

NEW DISCOVERIES
EVERY DAY

Sodwana pygmy seahorse

Scientists believe that about 90% of living species remain undiscovered. In fact, at least 200 new species are discovered every year. They are often hidden in remote places such as the Kubera cave, in the Eurasian country of Georgia, where nine species of spiders and the beetle *Duvalis abyssimus* were found. Other discoveries include the **Sodwana pygmy seahorse** (*Hippocampus nalu*), as small as a grain of rice; a mini shrimp called *Liropus minusculus*; and the **Caquetá titi** (*Plecturocebus caquetensis*), a tiny monkey.

Seas and forests continue to bring surprises like a new sunfish, the *Mola tecta*, the elegant **Emily's shrimpgoby** (*Tomiyamichthys emilyae*), and the **Tapanuli orangutan** (*Pongo tapanuliensis*) in Sumatra.

Emily's shrimpgoby

Pinocchio frog

For some of these new species, researchers have let their creativity run wild and given them names like *Neopalpa donaldtrumpi*, a moth measuring a fraction of an inch that sports a big blond tuft, or the **Skywalker hoolock gibbon** (*Hoolock tianxing*), discovered by Star Wars fans.

A little spider with a shape that resembles the Hogwarts sorting hat has been named *Eriovixia gryffindori*. The **Pinocchio frog** (*Litoria pinocchio*), with a funny nub on its nose, was discovered on Indonesia's Foja mountains.

By traveling down to the depths of the Mariana Trench (western Pacific Ocean), the *Pseudoliparis swirei*, a semi-transparent fish, has been discovered. The **okapi** *(Okapia johnstoni)* is another animal that many believed did not exist. Some 19th century explorers argued it was a zebra, others a strange donkey. . . . It was even thought to be fake, made by putting together the skins of giraffes, zebras, and horses! In 1986, it was finally identified as a relative of the giraffe and belonging to its own genus: *Okapia*.

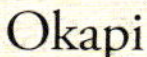

Okapi

The white **Yoda bat** (*Nyctimene albiventer*) has a double nose that makes it look like the wise master from the Star Wars movies that inspired its Western nickname. It was then renamed "hamamas tube-nosed fruit bat" after the Papuan word for "happy". The *Megalara garuda*, an Indian mega wasp, was so named in honor of Garuda, messenger of the gods.

There are 2-pound (0.9 kg) rodents able to open a coconut with their big teeth, the **Vangunu giant rat** (*Uromys vika*), and a small yet ravenous omnivore rodent, the **Sulawesi root rat** (*Gracilimus radix*), an endemic species of that island. In Congo, in 2007, two researchers ran into a **lesula** (*Cercopithecus lomamiensis*), a peaceful-looking monkey.

The majority of new discoveries are made up of animals that have been able to hide well: the *Typophyllum spurioculis* is a leaf-mimicking cricket; the female *Eulophophyllum kirki*, a katydid that looks like a pink tropical flower; or some snails, *Madrella amphora*, that pretend to be egg cocoons to hide from predators.

Yoda bat

The list is long and makes us hope that biodiversity can still surprise us. Some of these species have been discovered in Indonesia's primary forests and this helps us understand how important it is to preserve our unique, precious habitats.

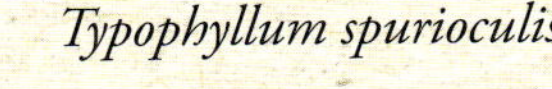

Typophyllum spurioculis

WHAT ABOUT TOMORROW?

Good news!

The initiatives for the protection of endangered animals—like controlling invasive species, wildlife preserves, rescue centers, the protection of habitats, and new laws—actually work! No less than 28 species of birds are not at risk anymore. Among them is the **Puerto Rican amazon** (*Amazona vittata*), a small parrot that dwindled to 13 individuals but now numbers 250. And there are now more than 700 **Przewalski horses** (*Equus ferus przewalskii*) grazing the Mongolian Steppe.

The **white rhinoceros** (*Ceratotherium simum*) is the largest land mammal after the elephant. For thousands of years people have hunted it for its horns because they believed they had healing powers. This has been proven wrong, and in fact, a rhinoceros' horn is made out of keratin, the same as our nails.

An international campaign was started in its defense, thanks to which funds have been raised to create special anti-poaching forces and several nature reserves. In the northern part of the white rhinoceros' range, efforts are underway to reintroduce this species to places where it has been absent for many years.

The **humpback whale** (*Megaptera novaeangliae*) is another success. It is a stocky whale with fins that are 13 to 15 feet (4 to 5 m) long (its scientific name actually means "big wings") and a big tail it uses as a propeller to do Olympic-style jumps and dives. As it loves to swim along coasts, it was hunted until its

number was reduced by 90%. Hunting the humpback was forbidden in 1955, and it is now of "least concern."

The **Andean mountain cat** (*Leopardus jacobita*) is a big cat with a thick, silver-grey coat and a long, ringed tail. It had almost been declared extinct when it was "captured" by camera traps while hunting some viscachas, its favorite food. It lives in four countries: Peru, Chile, Bolivia, and Argentina.

On the other hand, the **clouded leopard** (*Neofelis nebulosa*) might become extinct before scientists have a chance to study it more deeply. Little is known about it: it is solitary and hides in the impenetrable forests of Thailand, Indonesia, and Malaysia, ruthlessly hunted for its spotted fur, which looks like clouds.

There are still 6,500 mammals, 10,900 birds, 34,000 fish, and 1,000,000 insects, and a large number, as we have seen, are seriously at risk of extinction.

Let's advocate to save them all!

Index of Animals